"Of course, Britain could survive outside the EU... We could probably get access to the Single Market as Norway and Switzerland do..."

THE RT. HON. TONY BLAIR, MP - UK PRIME MINISTER,
SPEECH IN GHENT, 23RD FEBRUARY 2000

Contents

Introduction

For nearly forty years, Britain has been a member of the European Union (EU) and its forerunner organisations, the Common Market, European Economic Community (EEC) and European Community (EC). In that time, the protectionist pressures of the 1960s and 1970s which drove the UK to enter the EU Customs Union have been much reduced and the world environment has become more inclined to free trade, thanks primarily to the World Trade Organisation (WTO), formerly the General Agreement on Trade and Tariffs (GATT).

Despite this relaxation of the World economy and of tariff 'walls' to trade, the European Union (EU) has remained at heart undemocratic, protectionist, centralist and over bureaucratic. The EU has generated a red tape mountain that forces the member states to impose unacceptable burdens on their businesses and to make unwarranted and often damaging interventions in the lives of their citizens. This is not the British way but a Continental one which favours state control over personal liberty.

Supporters of the European Union try to scare British people into believing there is no alternative to British membership of the EU. They claim there is no 'Plan B' for Britain and we are fated, out of fear and a lack of confidence in our destiny, to remain with 'Plan A' – i.e. immersed within "an ever closer union" (as stated in the Treaty of Rome) to become a bit player with a diminished role within an emerging political superstate called the United States of Europe. Plan A has already led to Britain paying £50 million[1] a day in membership fees, imposed over 100,000 regulations and directives on us[2], and led to at least 50% (80% plus if German studies are to be believed) of our laws emanating from the EU[3].

Yet ever since joining the EC, a majority of the British population has expressed a wish to leave, particularly if an alternative trading relationship was proposed. An Angus Reid poll in July 2011, for example, found approximately 2 to 1 against staying in the EU:

49% would vote to leave the EU in a referendum; only 25% would vote to stay in, whilst 57% say EU membership has been negative for the UK; and only 32% believed it has been positive[4]. Support for withdrawal from the EU is the majority view, and that view is hardening. A You Gov Poll in August 2011 confirmed 52% of British citizens want to leave the EU, and just 30% want to stay in. A Guardian/ICM poll in October 2011 found that no less than 70% of voters now want an EU Referendum. Only 23% of the electorate would oppose such a vote.

The Ultimate Plan B argued for here is of a Britain replacing its membership of the European Union with a simple, free trading relationship under a UK/EU Free Trade Agreement.

A Free Trade Agreement (FTA) is a binding bilateral international agreement between sovereign countries and/or association of countries. The EU currently has 53 free trade or special trading agreements with countries all over the world, and is actively working for 74 more. Countries as diverse as South Korea, Morocco, South Africa, Chile and Mexico have Free Trade Relationships with the EU where their businesses can trade without the tariff barriers that were so prevalent in the past.

Under this Ultimate Plan B, Britain would negotiate a UK/EU Free Trade Agreement which conserves all the trade access EU membership currently provides but without the high cost of EU membership, and freeing Britain from the EU's political control, federalist ambitions and regulatory burden. It is not the same as the European Economic Area (EEA) or European Free Trade Area (EFTA), which are valuable alternatives but involve more EU control. This is a cross-party position: an independent Britain could be more Interventionist or more Free Market, but either way it will be a decision taken by the British people and not the EU.

The 'Positive Vision' outlined shows an alternative for Britain outside the EU that is credible, sustainable, positive and better for all. This booklet introduces a theme that will be contained in a later, far more comprehensive book on the subject.

We call for the British people to be granted an In/Out Referendum on membership of the European Union. Most people under the age of 53 have never had the chance to vote on the EU and those who voted in the 1975 referendum were misled about the political nature of the project and the true loss of sovereignty. The British people only ever wanted trade - not take over.

Summarised here is a plan for the future, a better future for all.

This is the Ultimate Plan B.

DAVID CAMPBELL BANNERMAN MEP

CHAPTER 1:

Why We Can Leave: The Top Ten EU Myths About Withdrawal Exposed

Myth 1: "Britain will lose three million jobs as a consequence of leaving the EU".

The Reality: If Britain leaves the EU it will put in place of its EU membership a UK/EU Free Trade Agreement to preserve the benefits of trade with the EU. The EU sells much more to us than we sell to them: in 2009, the UK's trade deficit in manufactured goods with the EU was £34.9 billion[5]. So, in theory, if there was the very worst case of a trade war and no trade at all with the EU, the UK would lose the three million jobs which depend on trade with the EU (10% of all UK jobs[6]), whilst the EU would lose some four million jobs[7]. This simply won't happen, as the EU would not want to lose their biggest customer. Even the Lisbon Treaty requires the EU to make a trade agreement with a nation that leaves the EU (under Article 50), and the EU already has these trade agreements with many of the world's nations including Switzerland and Norway.

"The UK has a huge visible trade deficit with the other members of the EU. It can fairly be concluded that the other EU states need us more than we need them".

SENIOR ECONOMIST RUTH LEA WRITING IN THE GLOBAL VISION PUBLICATION 'A NEW TRADING RELATIONSHIP FOR BRITAIN WITH THE EU'

Myth 2: "Britain will be excluded from trade with the EU by tariff barriers."

The Reality: The world has changed considerably since the UK joined in 1973. The EU has free trade agreements in place with 53 countries to overcome such tariffs and the UK/EU trade agreement would have no such tariffs, particularly if it merely replicated current EU membership arrangements. Indeed, the EU is very keen on free trade agreements for it is negotiating a further 74 such agreements and is seeking to open negotiations with an additional 12 countries[8].

The EU now exempts services and many goods from duties anyway. This meant that in 2009 the UK charged an average customs duty rate of only 1.76% on non-EU imports[9]. This is so low that it makes the EU Common Market, a customs union with tariff walls, pretty much redundant.

Article 50 of the Lisbon Treaty states that the Union shall negotiate and conclude an agreement with a state that exercises its freedom to withdraw from the Union.

Myth 3: "Britain cannot survive economically outside the EU in a world of trading blocs."

The Reality: Major economies such as Japan (the world's third largest) are not in trading blocs, but are very successful with international trade and global investment.

Nor is the EU the place where most economic growth is taking place: the EU's share of world's GDP is forecast to decline to 15% in 2020, down from 36% in 1980[10]. The EU is now more of a straightjacket than a life support machine to Britain.

The EU already has Free Trade Agreements with individual countries across the world, regardless of such trading blocs. Countries such as Norway and Switzerland are not in the EU, yet they export far more per capita to the EU than the UK does[11]. This suggests membership of the EU is not required for healthy trading relationships to exist between independent nation states and the EU.

In addition, Britain's best trading relationships are generally not with the EU but outside it - such as with the USA and Switzerland. The think tank Global Britain found that some 47% percent of UK exports go to the EU compared with 63% for Germany and 64% for France. However, 18% of British exports go to the US whereas for Germany, it is only 7%[12].

Indeed, the largest investor in the UK is not even an EU country - it is the USA. Furthermore, the latest UKTI Report 'Inward

Investment Report 2010/11' has found that the three top countries investing in the UK in terms of the numbers of projects are the non-EU countries of the USA, Japan and India. Moreover, the USA is the top destination for UK foreign investment[13]. In addition, Britain's exports to non-EU countries are surging ahead as these economies show high growth levels whilst the EU has been relatively sluggish.

Myth 4: "The EU is moving towards the UK's position on cutting regulations and bureaucracy."

The Reality: EU directives and regulations are subject to a 'rachet' effect – once they are in place they are highly unlikely to be reformed or repealed. Less than 10%[14] of Britain's GDP represents trade with the EU yet Brussels regulations afflict 100% of the UK economy; an economy which is the world's sixth largest[15]. More importantly, 80% of Britain's GDP is generated within the UK, such as Londoners buying Scottish whisky, so at least 80% (90% if trade to the Rest of the World is included) need not be subject to EU laws once the UK is free again.

UK Exports to the Rest of the World have been greater than UK exports to the EU since 2004.

2008 GLOBAL BRITAIN REPORT

In 2006, former Competition Commissioner Verheugen estimated that EU over-regulation alone costs some €600 billion per annum across the whole EU[16]. In 2010, Mats Persson of the Open Europe think tank stated EU regulation has cost Britain £124 billion since 1998[17]. This figure was based on the UK Government's official Impact Assessments of the cost to the UK of various EU Directives and Regulations.

Independent studies have put the net cost of the EU membership and its attendant 100,000 plus Directives and Regulations at between 4% and 10% of the UK's GDP[18]. A Treasury report in 2005 had four categories of EU costs which altogether came to 28% of Britain's GDP. Eliminating any possibility of any overlap between the Treasury's categories, the think tank Global Britain conservatively estimated that the likely EU cost was around 7% of UK GDP or £98 billion at 2009 prices[19]. In 2009, Matthew Elliot of the TaxPayers' Alliance estimated that EU membership is actually costing Britain £118 billion a year[20].

Whilst red tape savings are not direct cash savings, deregulation would result in a true "bonfire of regulations" that could fund either sizeable tax cuts or additional public spending, or a combination of the two.

Myth 5: "If we do leave, Britain will still have to pay billions to the EU and implement all its regulations but without any say in them."

The Reality: The UK has very little 'say' within the EU, and would have far more leverage outside the EU as an independent sovereign nation and the world's 6th largest economy.

The total cost of EU Regulations will be £356 billion by 2018.

SOURCE: OPEN EUROPE

The UK currently has only 8.4% of voting power 'say' in the EU[21], and the Lisbon Treaty ensured the loss of Britain's veto in many more policy areas. Britain's 72 MEPs are a minority within the 736 in the European Parliament (worsening to 73 out of 751 owing to Lisbon changes). The UK is increasingly losing influence within the EU and further EU enlargement, as with Turkey's 79 million citizens, would water it down further.

As for continuing EU contributions by an independent Britain, the Swiss and Norwegian examples show the UK would achieve substantial net savings. Official Swiss Government figures conclude that through their trade agreements with the EU, the Swiss pay the EU just under 600 million Swiss Francs a year but enjoy virtually free access to the EU market. The Swiss have estimated that full EU membership would cost Switzerland net payments of 3.4 billion Swiss francs a year[22].

Norway only had to make a few changes to its laws in order to make its products eligible for the European Union marketplace. In 2009, the Norwegian Mission to the EU estimated that Norway's total financial contribution linked to their EEA (European Economic Area) agreement is some 340 million Euros per year of which some 110 million Euros are contributions related to the participation in various EU programmes[23]. However, this is a fraction of the gross annual cost that Britain must pay for EU membership which is now £18.5 billion[24], or £50 million a day.

"The implementation of 3,000 EU legal acts has required only 49 changes of the law in Norway"

DOUGLAS CARSWELL MP & DANIEL HANNAN MEP IN THEIR BOOK 'THE PLAN'

Myth 6: "The EU has a positive impact on the British economy."

The Reality: British industries such as fishing, farming, postal services and manufacturing have already been devastated by Britain's membership of the EU.

EU membership costs the UK billions of pounds and large numbers of lost jobs thanks to unnecessary and excessive red tape, substantial membership and aid contributions, inflated consumer prices and other associated costs.

Britain will lose more jobs when such Directives as the EU's Alternative Investment Fund Managers Directive come into effect. This is already causing hedge fund and private equity markets to migrate elsewhere, doing substantial harm to financial services, responsible for 12% of the British economy[25] and 15% of income tax receipts[26].

"All told, the Common Fisheries Policy (CFP) had cost British coastal communities 115,000 jobs."

DR LEE ROTHERHAM IN HIS BOOK 'TEN YEARS ON: BRITAIN WITHOUT THE EUROPEAN UNION'

Myth 7: "The EU has brought Peace to the European Continent"

The Reality: Even now, the EU is only 27 nations out of the 47 European nations listed as national members of the Council of Europe. The forerunner of the EU, the Common Market, didn't even come into existence until 1958, and then only with 6 nations, and yet there was no war between European countries from 1945 to 1956 (Hungarian Revolution)[27]. Whilst peaceful international cooperation is welcomed at all levels, to say the EU is the sole guarantor of peace is an extreme exaggeration that is dishonest in its application.

It is NATO, founded in 1949 and dominated by the USA, and not the EU, that has actually kept the peace in Europe, together with parliamentary democracy. Both of these are being undermined by the EU. The former German President Herzog wrote a few years ago that "the question has to be raised of whether Germany can still unreservedly be called a parliamentary democracy.[28]" This was owing to the number of German laws emanating from the EU – which he assessed at some 84%[29].

One of the major tests of the EU's ability to keep the peace in Europe was the break up of Yugoslavia. It was the EU's interference that helped trigger a major civil war and its dithering that contributed to the deaths of some 100,000[30] people. It was only decisive action by US/NATO forces that stopped the violence, and peace was established by the US-brokered Dayton Agreement.

"I think this has been a European, not an American failure. The EC's decisions on the former Yugoslavia have been undermined by members of the EC themselves."

SHADOW FOREIGN SECRETARY JACK CUNNINGHAM SPEAKING TO THE INDEPENDENT IN JULY 1993

Myth 8: "Britain will lose vital Foreign Direct Investment (FDI) as a Consequence of Leaving the EU."

The Reality: In their 2010 survey on the UK's attractiveness to foreign investors, Ernst and Young found Britain remained the number one FDI destination in Europe owing largely to the City of London and the UK's close corporate relationship with the US[31]. EU membership was not mentioned at all in their table of key investment factors, which were (in order of importance): UK culture and values and the English language; telecommunications infrastructure; quality of life; stable social environment, and transport and logistics infrastructure. In any case, open access to the EU market would continue through a Free Trade Agreement in the manner of Switzerland and Norway whilst the UK would gain from higher growth, less regulation, more public spending and/or lower taxes and more suitable trade deals.

Myth 9: "Britain will lose all influence in the World by being outside the EU."

The Reality: Britain has a substantial 'portfolio of power' in its own right, which includes membership of the G20 and G8 Nations, a permanent seat on the UN Security Council (one of only five members) and seats on the International Monetary Fund (IMF) Board of Governors and World Trade Organisation (WTO). The UK also lies at the heart of the Commonwealth of 54 nations. Moreover, London is the financial capital of the world and Britain has the sixth largest economy. Last but not least, the UK is in the top ten manufacturing nations of the world[32].

Far from increasing British influence in the world, the EU is undermining UK influence. The EU is demanding there is a single voice for the EU in the United Nations and in the IMF, has made the British economy and City of London less competitive through overregulation, and negotiates more protectionist and less effective trade deals on behalf of the UK.

The new European External Action Service (EEAS) and its EU 'Foreign Minister' Baroness Ashton are undermining national diplomatic representation and the furtherance of British political and commercial interests through British embassies, which are being closed or downsized around the world. Foreign Office support for the BBC's World Service is being eliminated also. EU diplomats owe their allegiance to common EU interests and not British ones. Indeed EU diplomats are now claiming to have the right to speak for Britain on key issues such as security and defence - the EU Ambassador to the US Joao Vale de Almedia made such a claim in 2010[33].

The Commonwealth is increasingly being discriminated against by the EU policy on visas, so that non-EU Commonwealth citizens face having to obtain visas whilst citizens of even new EU entrants have automatic entry, and bonds with Britain are being lost.

Myth 10: "Legally, Britain cannot leave the EU."

The Reality: Technically, Britain could leave the EU in a single day. Legislatively, this would be achieved simply by repealing the European Communities Act 1972 and its attendant Amendment Acts through a single clause Bill passing through Westminster.

If the British people voted to leave in an In/Out Referendum or by voting in a party with EU withdrawal in its manifesto, Parliament would have to respect the will of the British people and there would be no justification for delay or obstruction in either House.

However, the process of setting up a replacement UK/EU Free Trade Agreement will take longer, though there would be no need for time-consuming negotiation of tariff reductions if the UK/EU Free Trade Agreement merely replicated existing EU trade arrangements.

"It is clear that there are no legal barriers to Britain's changing the terms of the relationship with the EU at all."

MARTIN HOWE QC WRITING IN THE GLOBAL VISION BOOKLET 'DEFINING A NEW RELATIONSHIP WITH EUROPE'

In addition, even the Lisbon Treaty's Article 50 enshrines the right of Member States to leave the Union, albeit in an unattractive manner. The same article requires the EU to seek a trade agreement with a member which leaves. Greenland established a precedent for a sovereign nation by leaving the EEC in 1985, and is prospering well outside of it. With Westminster still sovereign (for the moment), it is the British Parliament who will decide how and when Britain leaves the EU.

As the European Commission Treaties Office Database shows, an independent Britain will then be able to negotiate around many different types of EU association. Whilst France is a full EU member and Denmark is a full member with opt outs, Norway has an EU internal market association. On the other hand, Turkey has an EU Customs Union arrangement, while Switzerland has signed a free trade agreement. In contrast, Georgia has concluded a partnership and co-operation agreement, and Japan enjoys a 'Most Favoured Nation' status.

CHAPTER 2:

Why We Should Leave: The Top Ten Freedoms From Leaving The EU

By withdrawing from the European Union Britain would regain a whole host of positive and enabling freedoms that are denied to us by EU membership. The main freedoms are set out below:

1. Freedom to reassert British national sovereignty and control

Britain would take back control over its own destiny, defence, economy, foreign relations, environment, transport, fishing, farming and market controls - to name but a few.

UK democracy would be enhanced through the restoration of full national control to the British Westminster Parliament, ending the reality of between 50% and 80% of the UK's laws coming from the EU. Britain would no longer be subject to EU control through unelected EU Commissioners, bureaucratic diktats from Eurocrats, secret deals in the European Council, creeping EU-originated 'regionalisation' of Britain at the expense of counties, and the outvoting of its small group of MEPs in the European Parliament.

Britain would automatically negate the series of EU treaties involving huge transfers of sovereignty to the EU, from the Treaty of Rome through to the Lisbon Treaty. Their terms would cease to apply to the UK.

We would be free from increasing EU attempts to interfere in management of the British economy, despite not being in the Eurozone, such as proposals for the EU to vet British budgets before they are shown to the British people and plans to 'harmonise' taxes across the EU, such as with the EU-imposed Value Added Tax (VAT) and the proposed Financial Transactions Tax (FTT).

Britain would leave the European External Action Service (EEAS), which the House of Commons Library reports has at least 50 officials who are paid more than the Prime Minister, 7000 diplomats and civil servants and an agenda that competes with and undermines Britain's national and economic interests. Britain's embassies could be enhanced, and the BBC World Service safeguarded, out of the EU, to retain and build Britain's influence in the world and support international trade opportunities for UK companies.

The UK would cease to be an EU military partner through EU battle groups and EU-led military operations in the pursuit of a single EU military. Britain would maintain a strong independent defence capability whilst remaining a core member of NATO. The UK would be free to examine more international defence procurement, with the US or across the Commonwealth, rather than be a diminishing partner in French and German-dominated EU defence procurement.

Britain would be free to take back the 70% of European fishing waters it gave away to the EU, to replace the disastrous Common Fishing Policy with a sensible Norwegian-style fish management system and take control of the UK's territorial waters to the internationally recognised 200 nautical mile limit.

On farming, Britain would continue to pay farmers the same subsidies such as Single Farm Payments, but would be free to promote fairer prices and British produce through labelling for farmers, to eradicate quotas, such as those demanding imports of French milk, and ensure a level playing field in terms of high animal welfare standards applying to all produce sold in the UK market.

On transport, Britain could end EU moves to centralise control of transport within a Common European Transport Area and to force 'superlorries' onto UK roads (60 tonne trucks at 82 feet long[34]). Britain could require foreign lorries to pay a Swiss-style Vignette to use British roads (illegal under EU rules), enforce British safety standards on vehicles, hold down rail prices, liberalise ports regulation and take back national control of aviation safety.

2. Freedom to spend UK resources presently committed directly or indirectly through EU membership in the UK to the advantage of UK citizens

Leaving the EU would free up the direct 'membership' costs of £18.5bn a year, which equate to an annual net contribution of £10.3bn[35], and dramatically rising owing to Tony Blair's surrender of a sizeable part of the British rebate. Sums spent on regional aid could be spent in other ways determined by the UK Parliament rather than satisfying EU agendas, whilst farming subsidies should continue in their present form for as long as required within a fairer and freer agricultural regime.

This net contribution of £10.3bn p.a. could be spent, for example, on:

69 new hospitals a year (@£150m each)

412 new schools a year (@£25m each)

95 new bypasses a year (@£108m each)

A new high speed railway line network every 3 years (HS2 full proposal £32bn)

265,217 more police officers (@£38,836 average salary)

381,481 more nurses (@£27,000 average salary)

Income Tax cuts of 1p or a VAT cut of 1% a year

Halving the budget deficit within two parliaments.

Britain would also no longer be required to fund 'bailouts' of Eurozone nations, which it is liable for through the EU despite not even being in the Euro. However, it will still be liable for 4.5% of any bailout offered by the IMF[36]. By May 2011, the UK's total commitments had risen to £12.5bn for aid to Ireland, Greece and Portugal[37] but this amount will increase as a result of the second Greek bailout agreed in July 2011.

Britain would also be free of many hidden subsidies to the EU. For example, not included in the UK's membership contribution are the costs of subsidising EU students at British universities – where EU students are forbidden under EU laws from being charged international rates for tuition fees, which non-EU international students must pay. At Scottish Universities, English students will now be paying more than EU students.

Indirectly, the UK would benefit from scrapping or revising a mass of excessive or wasteful red tape generated by EU laws (see Chapter 4 and Freedom Point 5 below).

3. Freedom to control our national borders

Britain has given away control of immigration within the EU to the EU, and retains the power only to control non-EU immigration. This has led to huge disparities where Commonwealth citizens with family in Britain struggle to obtain visas whilst EU citizens with little link with the UK can automatically work here. It has also contributed to the largest ever inflows into the UK in our history, with the UK population rising by 4 million from 1997, which is only slightly less than the entire population of (Southern) Ireland moving to the UK in that timescale, and that figure is a net figure, which does not take into account the economic, social and cultural impacts of a mass outflow of British citizens to settle abroad. The British population used to be stable at around 58 million, and it is uncontrolled immigration that has driven the population up so rapidly to the current 62 million, with a forecast 70 million by 2027 *(ONS figures)*.

Leaving the EU will empower Britain to adopt a more balanced and more tightly controlled immigration policy, similar to the Australian visa-based system. This visa system could set down the number of visas available according to UK needs and the ability of public services, housing and infrastructure on a very crowded island to cope. It is likely that certain EU nation states will enjoy visa waiver schemes (in reality there is less need for visas with nations with comparative economic profiles such as France, Germany and Holland, the biggest inflows have been from former Communist states).

In the EU, all EU citizens have the right to move to the UK regardless of skill needs. This has resulted in the equivalent of a new city the size of York arriving every year[38]. With easier travel for North African countries and the prospect of Turkey's 79 million citizens being given the right to work in the EU, the scale of uncontrolled immigration is likely to worsen considerably unless the UK withdraws rapidly. Better controls over criminal elements coming into the UK, difficult under the EU's open door approach, can be enhanced too.

4. Freedom to restore Britain's special legal system

Britain would be able to restore traditional British justice by ending the overruling of British justice by foreign courts such as the EU's integrationist European Court of Justice (ECJ) and the European Court of Human Rights (ECHR) in Strasbourg, making the UK's Supreme Court genuinely supreme in the UK for all UK laws. Britain would also be free to leave the EU's Europol and Eurojust policing and justice systems.

British Justice would also be strengthened by withdrawing from the European Arrest Warrant (EAW), which is an abuse of traditional Habeas Corpus by allowing British citizens to be imprisoned for years abroad without trial, and by leaving the European Investigative Order (EIO) which turns our police into agents of foreign courts. Leaving will also free Britain from having to remain as a signatory to the European Convention of Human Rights (ECHR), which, while indeed being separate from the EU, Lisbon Treaty and EU membership rules still require Britain to sign up to. The UK will then be free to end the disgraceful enforcement of votes for prisoners and the widespread misuse of human rights claims made possible under the ECHR and UK Human Rights Act.

The UK could choose to codify long existing human rights under the Magna Carta and common law within its own Bill of Rights. EU citizens committing crimes in the UK may be deported more easily. Scottish law will also be restored alongside English law.

5. Freedom to deregulate EU's costly mass of laws

Examples of just some of the 100,000 EU regulations, directives and decisions are contained in Chapter 4. But the reality is with the UK now receiving between 50% and 80% of its laws from the European Union, the 'Mother of Parliaments' at Westminster has been effectively sidelined and undermined, and there has been a major loss of democratic control from the British nation state and UK citizens to the unelected, remote and unaccountable European Union, an institution whose accounts have not been signed off for 17 years in a row by its own Court of Auditors.

6. Freedom to make major savings for British consumers

Consumer prices have been driven up by EU membership, particularly energy bills through excessive environmental targets and the need to rebuild the UK National Grid and the majority of power stations, and by heavy subsidies to ineffective wind turbines. Above all, the costly EU emissions trading scheme costs families £117 per year[39].

Food prices are increased through requirements to take in expensive French agricultural produce and by the undermining of British farming. The cost of excessive red tape also feeds through to consumer prices across the board, and a reduction in red tape will bring price cuts over time.

7. Freedom to improve the British economy and generate more jobs

By stripping out reams of unnecessary red tape in the form of EU laws, such as the Working Time Directive, Agency Workers Directive and related excessive Health & Safety and Employment legislation which bear most heavily on small businesses, the lifeblood of jobs and the economy, the British economy will be stimulated and many more jobs will be created. Major plants producing steel, aluminium, chemicals and electrical power will be reprieved by the ending of excessive and unrealistic emissions targets.

Britain will also be free of EU State Aid provisions, unequally applied across the EU, so that if we choose to spend British taxpayers money saving a car industry (the EU prevented the UK saving Rover) or more post offices or the Royal Mail or helping a bank to survive, an unelected EU Commissioner will no longer have the power to veto such decisions. EU Procurement rules would also be removed, and the necessity to advertise UK contracts in the EU Journal.

Britain will also be able to return to 'Golden Shares' in major UK companies, banned under EU rules (except for defence companies), therefore enabling the UK Government to wield power where absolutely necessary to do so in order to safeguard British jobs and interests.

8. Freedom to negotiate better trade deals for Britain

Britain will be able to fill its 'empty chair' at the World Trade Organisation (WTO), where we are a member but cannot do any of our own trade deals now, as we have delegated to the EU the power to negotiate all trade deals on our behalf.

The EU is at heart more protectionist and interventionist than the UK. By taking back its right to negotiate the UK's own trade deals, the UK will be able to negotiate more suitable trade agreements with other nations, including emerging economies such as Brazil and China, and 13 of the fastest growing world economies in the Commonwealth. These trade deals will be more free trade and better tailored to the needs of the British economy and our exports. The deals would also be fairer to developing nations than the EU's semi-imperialist 'Economic Partnership Agreements' (EPAs), which have drawn withering criticism from developing nations, particularly in Africa and the Caribbean. They may promote trade rather than aid, helping the UK to scale back its development aid budget over time.

On the other hand, the countries of the Commonwealth will go from strength to strength. Currently, the Commonwealth numbers nearly two billion people and includes thirteen of the world's fastest growing economies. By 2015, the Indian middle class alone will number a staggering 267 million people[40]. Indeed, leading economist Willem Buiter of Citigroup predicts that India will supplant China to become the world's biggest economy in around 2050[41]. Free of EU membership, the UK will be able to seek far more advantageous globalised visions, for example, to pursue the concept of a Commonwealth Free Trade Area.

9. Freedom to save the NHS from EU threats to undermine it by harmonising healthcare across the EU, and to reduce welfare payments to non-UK EU citizens

Free of the EU, the UK will no longer have to comply with EU Directives moving healthcare towards a common European model at the expense of the NHS, which is very different from the more private insurance-based health system models in place in much of the EU.

The NHS will no longer be required to treat EU citizens without charge, only UK citizens. The Cross-Border Healthcare Directive which will open up the NHS to EU citizens across the Continent will also be subject to repeal.

Other relevant EU directives having severe impact on the NHS such as the Working Time Directive, which surgeons blasted as costing lives by undermining the British system of medical training, could now be removed. There could be an end to the disgraceful dumbing down of medical standards and exposure of British patients to under-qualified personnel forced by EU rules. In the past, this has led to such cases as Doctor Ubani and the overdose and death of a British patient. The Cambridgeshire North and East Coroner, William Morris, judged Dr Ubani to be 'incompetent' and the death was an 'unlawful killing'. The GMC confirmed that, in April 2011, a Spanish locum who had mistaken cancer for a sore thoat was struck off. In addition, there is a huge rise of EU nurses whose skills and ability to speak English are unknown thanks to EU rules banning proper competency checks on EU citizens[42]. This open door policy will be ended, putting organisations such as the General Medical Council back in control of British standards to protect patients.

On welfare, a move away from an 'EU-wide model' of EU citizens being common claimants would entitle the UK to cut back on welfare payments being made to non-UK citizens such as EU migrants claiming child benefit for their children who may never have lived in the UK. In 2010, some 32,000 non-UK citizens with children in other European countries were involved in this scam which costs the British taxpayer millions of pounds[43]. Moreover, British restrictions on claims from EU immigrants have been lifted at the likely additional cost of £2.5 billion a year following demands from the European Commission and the threat of legal action[44].

EU citizens would also lose their automatic right to claim UK welfare payments after three months residency[45]. As regards working in Britain, EU citizens would require visas to work except where a visa waiver scheme is agreed between the UK and a nation state, and these visas are likely to apply to poorer EU nations where there are large outflows to the UK to work. Visas would be awarded on the basis of UK needs, so that if there is an excess of supply for tradesmen, for example plumbers or builders, visas would not be awarded and some non-UK tradesmen may not be allowed to work in the UK.

10. Freedom to restore British customs and traditions

The EU has consciously or unconsciously sought to undermine notions and symbols of Britishness in the pursuit of harmonisation and an EU-wide identity. The mile, pint, hectare, and pounds and ounces have all been under threat, with only 'derogations' from Napoleon's system of metrification allowed (i.e. opt outs, often only for a short period before full compliance is required). The disgraceful persecution of the 'Metric Martyrs', one of whom died from the stress, for selling in time-honoured imperial measures, was an avoidable tragedy.

The Royal Mail is under threat, its proposed sell off being challenged by an EU State Aid inquiry focused on the transfer of pension payments to the State[46]. Post offices are closing owing to EU limits on State Aid. Meanwhile, major British businesses such as energy, airport, and rail freight companies are in the control of major EU companies, often to the cost of home grown talent, skills, status and opportunities abroad.

CHAPTER 3:

Why Leaving is Easy: The Step by Step Guide to Leaving the EU

In constitutional and legal terms, the Westminster Parliament is still sovereign. Therefore, Westminster need only repeal the 1972 European Communities Act (ECA) and its attendant European Amendment Acts for Britain to formally leave the European Union. The ECA is a short UK 'enabling act' (just 37 pages long), which enables the transfer of powers and sovereignty from the UK to the EU through a series of Amendment Acts. As such it is the spring for the river of the transfers of power to the EU.

A one clause Bill to repeal the ECA could be passed into law technically in a day if it is accepted by both the House of Commons and the Lords. However, this is a rare measure for an emergency Bill. Ordinarily, the longest that a Government Bill can be delayed by the House of Lords is one year. However, the Lords will feel unable to delay the Bill if the British people have already voted to leave in an In/Out Referendum. This will give the Government a very strong mandate and there will be little need for further debate, as that will have taken place already during the Referendum campaign.

The actual process of withdrawal from the EU would be similar to that proposed in the 1983 Labour Party General Election manifesto[47], once an 'Out' majority is secured in an In/Out Referendum. This is the most likely process of withdrawal:

Step 1:
The UK Government would announce an immediate halt to implementation of new EU Directives or enforcing new EU Regulations. The Government would open negotiations for a UK/EU Free Trade Agreement with the EU and the Government

would start the drafting of an ECA Repeal Bill. The UK financial contributions to the EU would continue for the moment.

Step 2:
The Repeal Bill would be introduced and passed by both Houses of Parliament, to become the Repeal Act. The Government would confirm that it would continue to honour Single Farm Payments and other EU payments such as regional grants to UK recipients until the Special Independence Budget is announced. A Draft UK/EU Free Trade Agreement would be produced. Government Departments and The Houses of Parliament would establish Deregulation committees on all the policy areas (empowered via the main Repeal Act) in order to begin the work of comprehensive deregulation.

Step 3:
The UK/EU Free Trade Agreement would be presented for approval to the UK Parliament and the EU. Once ratified by Westminster and the EU, Britain would then withdraw its representatives from the Council of Ministers, the European Parliament and from other EU Organisations. Financial contributions to the EU would cease at that point. Britain would have now formally left the EU.

Once free of the EU, the Government would be able to institute a series of important measures such as reasserting control over the UK's territorial waters, reinvesting sums earmarked for EU funding contributions to UK public spending or tax breaks in a Special Independence Budget; withdrawing recognition of the EAW; resuming Britain's seat on the WTO and pursuing negotiations for more advantageous free trade agreements between the UK and countries such as Brazil, India and China, and the wider Commonwealth.

Step 4:
The UK and the EU would agree to work together to bed down the new UK/EU Free Trade Agreement and maintain friendly relations. The Agreement would establish key areas of co-operation between Britain and the EU such as sea navigation, telecommunications

harmonisation, air safety control, as well as key legal principles such as the mutual respect for property and intellectual rights. The Agreement would also include 'transition' clauses which will be limited by time and would allow Britain to move smoothly from certain European provisions to its own standards over a number of years.

Following public consultation, the Deregulation Committees would present an ongoing series of repealing legislation to both Houses of Parliament. Each repealing Deregulation Act would have a timetable of implementation to allow citizens, organisations and businesses time to adjust to the changes. Each Government Department would set up their own Transition Committee to ensure the regulatory transition is as smooth and transparent as possible. The UK Government would introduce a Special Independence Budget and an 'Independence Fund' of reallocated EU membership and other costs, such as the gross contribution of £18.5bn p.a. (net contribution of £10.3bn p.a.) which will allow the reallocation of funds formerly dedicated to EU membership and other costs, and to pass on cost savings from deregulation to individuals and companies.

Once this procedure is complete, Britain will have restored full sovereignty and total control over British laws to the British people and their representatives in Westminster. Moreover, the relationship with the EU would now be mutually beneficial as it will be based on friendly trade, not political control by a remote, unaccountable EU bureaucracy.

CHAPTER 4:

How Leaving Can Free Britain from the EU Regulatory Burden – Some Examples

There are well over 100,000 EU regulations, directives and decisions that have legal force in the UK. These EU laws cost billions and act to destroy jobs, hold the British economy back and drive up costs. Here are 10 examples out of these 100,000, to give a flavour of some of the EU Directives that dispel the myth the EU is just about trade and demonstrate that it has affected every aspect of our daily lives from bin collections to light bulbs, passport controls to the administration of justice, tuition fees to health services.

All of these directives and regulations, the body of law ('acquis communautaire') that the EU makes mandatory on members, could be removed or amended in a free Britain, for all but some 10% of the economy accounted for by trade with the EU. At present there is no escape.

1 The EU Working Time Directive 2003/88/EC

This Directive limits the EU working week to 48 hours. The UK negotiated an opt-out from full implementation of the law, providing an agreement is reached between private employers and employees. Despite this, the UK has been forced progressively to extend the 48-hour working week to public sector employees and the NHS.

This has had a dire effect on the NHS in particular. Senior doctors have warned that rules on working time are hindering care in the NHS[48]. The European Parliament is now proposing to extend the full 48-hour working week to all British professions. Open Europe estimates that full implementation of the Working Time Directive in the UK will cost British businesses £11.9bn a year[49], nearly equivalent to the entire increased foreign aid budget.

2 The Agency Workers Directive 2008/104/EC

The UK implementation of the EU Directive on Agency Workers is another EU working time law. After a 12-week qualifying period, temporary and agency workers will be entitled to the same working conditions as full time workers, extending rights to pay, holiday and insurance (if offered). In the drawing up of the Directive, the CBI warned that 250,000 jobs were at stake[50], even risking the economic recovery[51]. Open Europe estimated that 8 out of 10 people affected by this Directive will be in the UK.

The Government's own Impact Assessment report found that the Directive will impose £3.7bn of preparatory costs on British business, with an annual cost of £1.9bn[52]. This is precisely what British businesses or workers do not need in tough economic times.

3 The Landfill Directive 1999/31/EC

Under the Landfill Directive, EU member states have targets to meet on recycling biodegradable waste. If they don't meet these targets, member states are fined substantially and directly. While the aim of recycling is laudable, the means of aggressive fining and unrealistic targets is rigid, expensive and undemocratic.

The Local Government Association estimates these fines could push up council tax bills by as much as £50, with a total national cost of £1.1bn[53]. In addition, councils started introducing fortnightly bin collections as a way of complying with the targets[54] in the Directive which is why the EU is responsible for rises in illegal dumping[55] and their attendant health and vermin problems. It was EU rules that initially prevented the Government reintroducing weekly bin collections, as promised.

4 The Postal Services Directives 1997/67/EC, 2002/39/EC, 2008/6/EC

The EU has seized control of postal services through a series of three directives that broke up national postal services and have helped to undermine the Royal Mail. Whilst helping competitors, the legislation still requires national postal services to provide a minimum, universal service, but one based on the Continental post which is worse than the traditional UK minimum service. In the UK, the profit-making business bulk mail sectors were sold off, while the loss-making element of hand delivery of letters was left in Royal Mail's hands.

To make matters worse EU rules on State Aid, which prevent State funding that may create so-called 'unfair competition', stopped the Government funding many post offices and led to mass closures. As things stand the UK government has to obtain permission from the European Commission for payments to the Post Office[56], rules which prevented the government putting more money into the Post Office Network to save sub post offices, many being rural.

EU intervention is now threatening the salvation of the Royal Mail through the Government's sell off plans. The EU Competition Commissioner has launched an 'in-depth' investigation into these plans on the grounds that the State taking on pension liabilities of £8 billion[57] and restructuring debt constitutes unacceptable 'State Aid' under EU rules allegedly initiated by certain competitor mail services owned by other EU governments.

5 The EU Large Combustion Plant Directive 2001/80/EC

As part of EU-driven environment policy, the EU has compelled all member states to heavily regulate combustion plants, with dire consequences for European energy supplies. The Large Combustion Plant Directive requires all combustion with a thermal input equal to or more than 50MW to either have to fit expensive filters or close[58].

Even if the claimed aims are welcome, the actual effects for the UK are dangerous, with the UK estimated to lose a third of its national energy use by 2020, meaning Britain will either have to spend more importing fuel from unstable regions of the world or risk overdependence on renewable energy that, as the Renewables Directive shows, is too intermittent in supply and doesn't provide value for money[59]. In short, the lights could go out in Britain.

6 EU Environment Directives: Renewables Directive 2009/28/EC & Bio Fuel Directive 2003/30/EC

The EU Renewables Directive sets down an EU-wide target for 20% of energy to come from renewable sources by 2020[60]. The UK target is to reach 15% as part of the EU-wide goal. Through leaked UK Government (dti) documents, the government estimated the 15% goal would cost between £5bn and £11bn per year, which is the equivalent of between £330 and £730 per family in the UK. Were the UK to reach 20% of renewable energy, the cost could rise to £22bn[61] a year. The latest preference for a 30% target is uncosted at present.

Open Europe estimated that to reach this 15% goal, between two and three wind turbines will have to be built in the UK every day until 2020, despite the fact that wind power only works between 20% and 40% of the time[62] ('operational capacity'), and some turbines work for less than 10%.

Cambridge University Electricity Policy Research Group has found that UK households will each end up paying some £90 per year for the cost of wind turbines and other kinds of renewable energy. These costs are part of the Government plan to reach its renewable energy targets.

It is thought that the UK's National Grid will also need to be rebuilt to cope with wind power surges and the varied output from renewables, adding yet further to people's energy costs[63]. This is all part of a £100bn environmental plan[64]. Such is the scale of decision-making and massive financial liabilities included here that it is essential for British citizens to decide on these directly through the Westminster Parliament and not have them foisted upon us from the undemocratic EU.

The Bio Fuel Directive set a target for bio fuels to make up 5.75% of transport fuel by the end of 2010, despite biofuels proving to actually harm the environment. In 2008, the UK parliamentary Environmental Audit Committee called for a moratorium on agricultural produce used for fuel (agrofuels) due to concerns over food price inflation and current methods of fuel-crop production that require considerable amounts of fossil fuel to produce bio fuel[65]. A 2009 Times report found that bio fuel targets had cost British-based oil companies £100 million in refinery modernisation[66].

Open Europe estimated that the directive and consequently rising biofuel demand will increase annual food prices per family by between £200 and £260 a year which will hit struggling families hard[67].

7 The EU Citizens' Directive 2004/58/EC

This Directive effectively gave overall control of the UK's Borders and Immigration policy to the EU. It gives anyone in the EU, and their dependants, regardless of nationality, the right to live and work in any other EU member state. Given the huge disparities between EU nations in terms of wealth and services, more advanced nations such as the UK attract a disproportionate number of migrants, but without the means of management and control of numbers whilst we remain a member of the EU.

Whilst provisions in the directive allow restrictions on the basis of public policy, security or health, successive UK governments have refused to limit new immigration from the expanded EU. This is in spite of the fact that millions of British people are on the dole or facing redundancy, and such moves can cause undesirable community tensions.

8 The EU Data Retention Directive 2006/24/EC

This directive compels all internet service providers to store all communication information for a year. The privacy issues here are compelling, especially as the UK government will be able to apply, through the security services, for individual pieces of information.

Privacy group Statewatch has said that mandatory data retention will effectively place everyone's emails and postings under surveillance[68]. Open Democracy has criticised the ease with which third parties could abuse such private information obtained through data retention[69]. The Open Rights Group has said that data retention endangers society's open communication and dialogue[70]. Moreover, the UK government lost millions of pieces of private (HM Revenue and Customs) data in 2007[71], and other sensitive data has been lost on a consistent basis.

9 The Alternative Investment Fund Managers Directive and other Financial Services Directives 2004/39/EC and 2009/39/EC

The Alternative Investment Fund Managers Directive (AIFM) now regulates the practices of all EU-based Alternative Investment Fund Managers (rather than funds themselves). As with the Agency Workers Directive, this law hurts the UK disproportionately as the UK is home to 23% of the EU's AIF Management Companies whilst international law firm Osborne Clarke estimates that 80% of European hedge fund managers are actually based in the UK[72]. Forcing more regulation - such as dictating how much can be borrowed, requiring AIFMs to only deal with EU clients and restricting who AIFMs can bank with - will not only cost the UK economy £5.3bn (according to Open Europe) but could cost the UK 18,000 jobs[73]. A report in February 2011 found a 29% increase in British citizens working in financial services in non-EU Switzerland, which has full access to the EU market without having to apply these directives[74].

This is just a part of the EU's 'power grab' over regulation of the British financial services industry, which accounts for 12% of UK GDP. The EU has suddenly moved to legislate in financial service areas such as the creation of EIOPA, the European Insurance and Occupational Pension Authority. EIOPA joins the European Securities and Markets Agency (ESMA) and the European Banking Agency (EBA) as the EU's financial regulators. Most regulation of the City of London, the world's leading financial centre, has sought to advantage competitive EU centres such as Frankfurt and Paris, but in effect loses business to non-European centres in the Middle and Far East. Under threat too are billions in tax revenue needed to fund hard-pressed UK public services.

10 The EU Investigation Order Directive 2010/0817 (COD) and related European Arrest Warrant Council Framework Decision 2002/584/JHA

These draft proposals, which the UK opted into in 2010, include plans for member states to order police and criminal investigations within other member states regardless of whether a certain act is a crime in that member state. This development is a massive transfer of power without a referendum.

Giving other EU member states the power to direct British police forces as agents of foreign courts places a huge burden on our police whilst not ensuring we can hold the decision makers in other EU member states to account. Rights groups such as Statewatch[75] and Fair Trials International have voiced strong concerns about the EIO, calling it "a measure that has serious implications for stretched police forces and civil liberties"[76].

This is in addition to the existing European Arrest Warrant (EAW) legislation, a law intended to secure the conviction of terrorists and cross-border criminals which, sadly, has infringed individual liberties and gone way beyond its intended scope. The EAW regards all EU legal systems as equally good and British judges are denied the opportunity to look at the 'prima facie' evidence, normal under former extradition processes.

For example, in June 2011 Andrew Symeou, who had been extradited to Greece under the European Arrest Warrant and held for a year in a Greek prison prior to trial, was found not guilty of the charges he was extradited on[77]. The lack of evidence required for extradition will be likely to give other EU governments carte blanche to order investigations in the UK, with no safeguards by British judges to protect British people from overzealous actions.

CHAPTER 5:

Frequently Asked Questions

Q1: Britain can't survive 'out on its own' can it? We need to be in the EU club of nations or we'll eventually become the 51st US State?

A1: It is a false choice to think the only alternatives for the UK are to be in the EU or be the 51st US State. Non-EU countries such as Norway and Switzerland enjoy prestigious international roles, prosperous economies and a wide range of free trade agreements with other countries. However, they aren't members of the EU and no-one has ever claimed that they must join the US in order to survive.

With the sixth largest economy in the world, a permanent seat on the UN Security Council, membership of the G8, G20, WTO and the IMF, and close ties with the 54 nations of the Commonwealth, Britain will flourish by being out of the EU as it will be able to represent and protect its interests much better than from within the ineffectual and bureaucratic EU.

Q2: Surely Britain can't leave the EU now anyway, can it?

A2: Yes it can. Britain is a sovereign nation (for the present) and can choose to leave the EU simply by repealing Ted Heath's European Communities Act 1972. Britain's right to leave the EU is also enshrined in Article 50 of the Lisbon Treaty which lays down the process for a member state to quit the Union. Moreover, there is historical precedent as Greenland left the EEC in 1985.

Q3: Don't we have to be in the EU as half our trade is with the EU?

A3: 'Half our trade' does not mean 'half our economy'- let's get it in proportion. Most British trade is within Britain – 80% of our economy is British citizens and businesses buying British goods and services. 20% of our economy depends on international trade; and half of that (around 10%) is trade with the EU. Britain is increasingly trading more with the Rest of the World than with the EU[78].

Non-EU member countries such as Norway and Switzerland enjoy very beneficial trading relationships with the EU thanks to their free trade agreements. On leaving the EU, Britain would secure a similar, if not better, free trade agreement with the EU as its biggest customer and a major world economy. Our trading position will benefit from reduced regulation and taxes, and more appropriate free trade agreements with other countries.

In addition, the EU export figures are skewed upwards by the 'Rotterdam-Antwerp Effect' and the 'Netherlands Distortion'. This is where UK exports to non-EU countries sent via a transhipment centre such as Rotterdam are counted as exports to the EU, even though their ultimate destination is not in the EU[79].

Q4: Don't the benefits of being in the EU outweigh the costs of membership?

A4: There are no benefits of being in the EU that could not be achieved through a Free Trade Agreement and friendly international relations, and without the ever increasing membership cost. Switzerland estimates that they currently pay just under 600 million Swiss francs for access to EU markets but EU membership would cost them net payments of 3.4 billion Swiss francs. British Governments of all colours consistently refuse to do a similar cost benefit analysis of British membership of the EU, claiming that the benefits are 'self evident'[80].

On the other hand, Britain pays £50 million a day to the EU in gross contributions for the privilege of membership while the cost burden of the EU's 100,000 plus directives and regulations is estimated to cost billions of pounds. Last but not least, EU membership has devastated entire British industries such as fishing and aluminium production, and others will surely follow if we remain in the EU.

EU membership carries no tangible benefit but costs us billions of pounds and tens of thousands of jobs. This is why we must leave immediately.

Q5. If we leave the EU, then won't we lose all the money that the EU gives us such as regional grants and support for farmers?

A5: But it's our (your) money anyway! These payments come in a large part from the British taxpayer, from funds paid to the EU, with a smaller and smaller proportion being recycled back to us. Britain pays in £18.5 billion a year, and receives back some £3 billion in CAP farming payments[81] and should receive back some £6.7 billion total over seven years from 2007-13 in regional aid payments[82]. The net contribution to the EU is now some £10.3 billion a year.

British farmers will continue to be paid single farm payments and the same subsidies up until the point they do not need these subsidies owing to more favourable domestic prices and/or a better business environment. Regional grants could continue to be paid but in a form determined by Westminster not the remote, undemocratic EU.

Q6: I would like the chance to live and work in other EU nations. Don't we lose this right to work if we leave the EU?

A6: No. Norwegian and Swiss citizens are not in the EU but have the right to work in the EU as part of their trade agreements with the EU. Britain can secure the same rights within a UK/EU Free Trade Agreement so that UK citizens will retain the right to work in other EU nations.

But as a result of this change, there will also be many more job opportunities in the UK as the British Government will now be free to restrict immigration from the EU through a visa system similar to that currently applied to non-EU citizens. Currently, over a million EU nationals work in the UK compared to some 287,600 Britons who work in the EU[83]. This imbalance does affect the British unemployment rate.

Independence from the EU means that the British Government will have the power and freedom to reserve more British jobs for British people, but not at the cost of losing the right to work in other EU countries. This will be of most benefit to young people who have been hardest hit by the recession.

Q7: Wouldn't leaving the EU be a terrible shock? Surely Britain's economy would suffer even more if we left the EU?

A7: No. There will be very little difference in feel after withdrawal, just as Norway and Switzerland now feel European whilst being outside the EU. 'Normal life' would continue after withdrawal. British citizens would continue to travel normally within the EU, British businesses to trade normally with the EU, and British workers to work normally in the EU.

Over time the economy would benefit from withdrawal through lower taxes and/or more public spending, reduced national debt, lower consumer prices, reduced business regulation, enhanced job and trade opportunities, better trade deals and reduced mass immigration into the UK with its pressures on housing and public services.

Q8: I think The EU does some good things – such as on the environment and over social legislation. Won't all these be lost if we left the EU?

A8: No. It would be up to the British Parliament and British people to decide what EU legislation they wished to keep, remove, emulate or even enhance – but the decision would be democratic and be made in the UK and not by a remote, undemocratic, unaccountable EU bureaucracy. The debate over whether EU environmental, social or other measures were good or bad would be conducted where it should be – in Westminster. If EU legislation was judged to be beneficial under the proposed comprehensive deregulation exercise post withdrawal, it could be retained and even added to. In contrast, the UK would also be free to mirror future EU legislation if it judged this to be positive to British interests. But the UK would cease to be compelled to accept the 100,000 plus EU directives and regulations.

Q9: Don't you just want to leave the EU because you don't like foreigners?

A9: Absolutely not. The EU is not the same as Europe. Europe is 47 nations not just the 27 members of the EU, and wanting to be an independent nation state does not in any way mean you dislike Europe or Europeans. This is a falsehood created by those who clearly have no credible arguments to justify Britain's continuing membership of the EU. The arguments against the European Union centre around it being a remote, undemocratic bureaucracy, but everyone is in favour of friendly relations with Europe, and trading freely. Britain should follow the example of countries such as Switzerland and Norway who are at the heart of Europe but are not members of the EU, for sound democratic, common sense and budgetary reasons, not because they don't like foreigners.

Britain would continue as an international, globalised nation but with the ability to control migrant flows into the UK based on a fair and reasonable visa system.

Q10: Will leaving the EU mean the United Kingdom is more likely to break up, since nations such as Scotland and Wales seem more pro-EU than England?

A10: No, quite the reverse. Before Britain joined the EU in 1973, nations such as Scotland were strongly pro the British Union, which provided substantial investment and support for the home nations (and still does). For example, Scotland had more (Conservatives and) Unionist MPs in the 1950s than Labour, but the Scottish Conservative Party has just one MP in Scotland now. The European Union has acted to compete with and undermine the British Union, with national independence parties encouraged to believe they could be successful as a separate EU nations, with their own commissioners, despite Brussels still remaining in charge whether they remain in the UK or not.

The UK will also be less likely to break up because any home nation leaving an independent UK would have to reapply to join the EU and meet its criteria for entry, and would risk being vetoed in its application by any EU nation state concerned at its own separatist movements – Spain with the Basques, Italy with the Northern League, for example, or by those unwilling to take on subsidies for new EU members.

In 2004 the then President of the European Commission Romano Prodi stated that a newly independent state must apply for membership in its own right rather than inherit any existing membership. This means that any member country has the right to object to Scotland's (and other nation state's) membership applications[84].

Author

David Campbell Bannerman is a Conservative MEP for the East of England. He created the 'Positive Vision' programme to illustrate in a positive, factual, and balanced way how Britain could flourish by leaving the European Union.

Elected as an MEP for the Eastern Counties in 2009 for UKIP, Mr Campbell Bannerman served with UKIP for seven years as Party Chairman, Deputy Leader and Head of Policy before returning to the Conservative Party in 2011. He previously served for 20 years with the Conservatives, including in Government as a Special Adviser on the Northern Ireland Peace Process; as a Ministerial Transport Adviser; as Chairman of the influential Bow Group think tank when it had 100 MP members; and as a Westminster candidate and local councillor. David has held a number of high profile communications roles in the private sector, both in-house and through leading agencies.

His hobbies include writing film screenplays, country walks and an interest in industrial heritage.

Acknowledgements:

With thanks to the MEP Research and support team: Niall Stewart, Tim Aker, Olly Adam, Sheila Brown, and Peter Reeve.

To the Freedom Association for their encouragement and support.

To the ECR Group for facilitating publication of this paper.
Note: the views expressed are personal to the Author and do not represent the official views of the ECR Group, nor that of the Conservative Party.

References

1 Daily Mail 24th November 2011 - www.dailymail.co.uk/news/article-2065462/Were-paying-50m-day-EU-Britains-contribution-Brussels-rises-18-5bn.html
and
ONS Pink Book 2011 - Table 9.1

2 www.timesonline.co.uk/tol/news/world/article395139.ece

3 www.parliament.uk/briefingpapers/commons/lib/research/rp2010/RP10-062.pdf - How much legislation comes from Europe? - Commons Library Research Paper

4 www.angus-reid.com/wp-content/uploads/2011/07/2011.07.12_EU_BRI.pdf

5 http://services.parliament.uk/hansard/Lords/ByDate/20101125/writtenanswers/part052.html

6 www.bbc.co.uk/news/business-12757675 (Note: The BBC quoted ONS statistics that there were 29.16 million in work. Three million jobs therefore represents 10% of the total)

7 Global Vision - UK-EU Trade creates far fewer jobs in the uk than in the rest of the EU by Ruth Lea

8 EU Trade European Commission – Overview of FTA and Other Trade Negotiations - trade.ec.europa.eu/doclib/docs/2006/december/tradoc_118238.pdf

9 Global Britain Briefing Note No. 70

10 http://blogs.telegraph.co.uk/news/danielhannan/100045697/why-europe-rose-and-why-it-is-now-declining

11 Global Britain Briefing Note No. 62

12 Global Britain Briefing Note No. 66

13 UK Trade and Investment Key Facts August 2010

14 Global Britain Briefing Note No. 67 – The official figure of 11.1% is too high as this includes the Rotterdam-Antwerp Effect and the Netherlands Distortion.

15 www.buyusa.gov/uk/en/uk_commercial_guide.html

16 www.openeurope.org.uk/research/singlemarketbriefing.pdf

17 www.openeurope.org.uk/media-centre/pressrelease.aspx?pressreleaseid=135

18 Global Britain Briefing Note 65 quotes studies – A Cost Too Far by Ian Milne and other studies

19 www.globalbritain.org/BNN/BN65CostofEUmembership.pdf

20 www.telegraph.co.uk/news/worldnews/europe/6198708/EU-costs-Britain-118bn-a-year.html

21 QMV - http://europa.eu/institutions/inst/council/index_en.htm (29 UK votes divided by 345 total number of votes) x 100 equals 8.4%
and
www.openeurope.org.uk/research/EUsupervisors.pdf

22 Swiss Confederation - Federal Department of Foreign Affairs – Bilateral Agreements Switzerland - EU report

23 www.eu-norway.org/ARKIV/newsarchives/EEA_agreement_facts

24 Daily Mail 24th November 2011 - www.dailymail.co.uk/news/article-2065462/Were-paying-50m-day-EU-Britains-contribution-Brussels-rises-18-5bn.html
and
ONS Pink Book 2011 - Table 9.1

25 http://ukinchina.fco.gov.uk/en/business/help-for-uk-companies/Country-information/UKStrengthinFinancialServices/

26 www.telegraph.co.uk/finance/newsbysector/banksandfinance/8673105/City-job-cuts-to-cost-the-Government-1.3bn-in-lost-tax-revenue.html

27 http://en.wikipedia.org/wiki/List_of_conflicts_in_Europe#1945-1989 and news.bbc.co.uk/1/hi/world/europe/5379586.stm

28 http://euobserver.com/9/23250

29 www.openeurope.org.uk/research/outofcontrol.pdf

30 The Guardian reported 100,000 dead in Bosnian civil war in 2008 - www.guardian.co.uk/world/2008/jul/22/warcrimes.balkans1

31 Ernest & Young Press Release dated 2nd June 2010 - www.ey.com/UK/en/Newsroom/News-releases/GOV---10-06-02---UK-tops-European-inward-investment-league
and
www.ey.com/Publication/vwLUAssets/2010_UK_attractiveness_survey/$FILE/EY_2010_UK_attractiveness_survey.pdf -Graph 3.8

32 www.guardian.co.uk/business/2011/aug/15/manufacturing-recession-trade-deficit

33 www.telegraph.co.uk/news/worldnews/europe/eu/7941313/New-EU-ambassador-in-Washington-claims-transatlantic-authority.html

34 www.dailymail.co.uk/news/article-1352330/Get-ready-60-tonne-lorries-new-EU-plans.html

35 Daily Mail 24th November 2011 - www.dailymail.co.uk/news/article-2065462/Were-paying-50m-day-EU-Britains-contribution-Brussels-rises-18-5bn.html
and
ONS Pink Book 2011 - Table 9.1

36 www.telegraph.co.uk/finance/financialcrisis/8586852/How-much-could-Britain-pay-to-bail-out-Greece.html

37 www.express.co.uk/posts/view/247165

38 www.statistics.gov.uk/cci/nugget.asp?id=260
and
www.york.gov.uk/environment/Planning/Local_development_framework/LDF_Evidence_base/MYEforYork/

39 www.taxpayersalliance.com/home/2009/10/new-research-emissions-trading-scheme-costs-consumers-3-billion-a-year.html

40 http://articles.economictimes.indiatimes.com/2011-02-06/news/28424975_1_middle-class-households-applied-economic-research

41 http://money.msn.com/how-to-invest/dispatch.aspx?post=7b5c156c-f0eb-4c70-b3db-9619ce096ec8

42 www.dailymail.co.uk/health/article-1366620/Number-foreign-NHS-nurses-doubles-amid-fears-dont-know-language.html

43 www.guardian.co.uk/politics/2011/jun/13/clampdown-uk-benefits-foreign-nationals

44 www.dailymail.co.uk/news/article-1315735/EU-warns-Britain-stop-thousands-migrants-claiming-welfare-handouts.html
and
http://www.migrantsrights.org.uk/blog/2011/05/restrictions-a8-nationals-lift-last

45 www.dailymail.co.uk/news/article-1362451/100k-Eastern-European-migrants-free-claim-UK-benefits-EU-ruling.html

46 www.cwuplymouthandeastcornwall.org/2011/08/european-commission-opens-investigation-into-royal-mail-state-aid/

47 www.labour-party.org.uk/manifestos/1983/1983-labour-manifesto.shtml (and) www.politicsresources.net/area/uk/man/lab83.htm

48 www.timesonline.co.uk/tol/life_and_style/health/article6869585.ece

49 www.openeurope.org.uk/research/wtdoptout2.pdf

50 www.personneltoday.com/articles/2007/09/17/42375/agency-workers-directive-a-new-push-on-the-legislation-controlling-temporary-workers-rights.html

51 www.telegraph.co.uk/finance/jobs/8723731/New-EU-job-rights-will-derail-British-recovery.html

52 www.berr.gov.uk/files/file53058.pdf

53 http://new.lga.gov.uk/lga/core/page.do?pageId=4686690

54 http://news.bbc.co.uk/1/hi/uk_politics/6898050.stm

55 www.dailymail.co.uk/news/article-453965/Minister-admits-fortnightly-rubbish-collections-increase-fly-tipping-councils.html

56 http://ec.europa.eu/eu_law/state_aids/comp-2007/n388-07.pdf

57 www.parliament.uk/briefing-papers/SN04940.pdf

58 europa.eu/legislation_summaries/environment/air_pollution/l28028_en.htm

59 http://www.telegraph.co.uk/comment/columnists/benedict-brogan/7309946/Labour-has-pushed-us-to-the-brink-of-a-blackout.html

60 www.euractiv.com/en/energy/eu-renewable-energy-policy-linksdossier-188269

61 www.openeurope.org.uk/research/dtileakedpaper.pdf

62 www.independent.co.uk/news/science/breezy-does-it-how-wind-turbines-work-1862393.html
and
http://business.timesonline.co.uk/tol/business/industry_sectors/natural_resources/article6981585.ece

63 http://business.timesonline.co.uk/tol/business/movers_and_shakers/article3872382.ece

64 news.bbc.co.uk/1/hi/uk/7467336.stm

65 www.parliament.uk/parliamentary_committees/environmental_audit_committee/eac_210108.cfm

66 www.timesonline.co.uk/tol/news/environment/article6101744.ece

67 www.openeurope.org.uk/research/environmenttargets.pdf

68 www.statewatch.org/eu-data-retention.htm

69 www.opendemocracy.net/blog/ourkingdom-theme/ourkingdom/2009/02/15/eu-data-retention-directive-endangers-democracy

70 www.openrightsgroup.org/blog/2008/fighting-the-data-retention-directive

71 www.timesonline.co.uk/tol/news/uk/article2907495.ece

72 www.osborneclarke.com/~/media/Files/publications/import/en/new-european-directive-proposes-extensive.ashx

73 www.openeurope.org.uk/research/aifmd.pdf

74 www.moneyweek.com/blog/how-much-the-50-per-cent-tax-rate-is-costing-britain-00321

75 www.statewatch.org/analyses/no-96-european-investigation-order.pdf

76 www.fairtrials.net/news/article/uk_opts_into_controversial_european_investigation_order_law/

77 www.bbc.co.uk/news/uk-england-london-13810608

78 www.globalbritain.org/BNN/BN68GrowthExportsImports%5B1%5D.pdf

79 www.globalbritain.org/BNN/BN64RotterdamAntwerpNethDistortion.pdf

80 http://hansard.millbanksystems.com/lords/1995/jul/05/eu-costs-and-benefits-of-membership

81 www.telegraph.co.uk/earth/agriculture/8451261/Reform-of-farm-subsidies-risk-putting-UK-farmers-out-of-business-MPs.html

82 www.helm.org.uk/upload/pdf/European-Funding6.pdf?1313128316

83 www.telegraph.co.uk/news/election-2010/7679514/General-Election-2010-Labour-accused-of-misleading-voters-over-EU-migration.html

84 http://thescotsman.scotsman.com/politics/EU-president-deals-blow-to.2520616.jp